Stay Safe!

Fire Safety

Sue Barraclough

www.heinemann.co.uk/library
Visit our website to find out more information about Heinemann Library books.

To order:
☎ Phone 44 (0) 1865 888066
🖹 Send a fax to 44 (0) 1865 314091
🖥 Visit the Heinemann Bookshop at www.heinemann.co.uk/library to browse our catalogue and order online.

First published in Great Britain by Heinemann Library, Halley Court, Jordan Hill, Oxford OX2 8EJ, part of Pearson Education. Heinemann is a registered trademark of Pearson Education Ltd.

Editorial: Diyan Leake and Cassie Mayer
Design: Joanna Hinton-Malivoire
Illustration: Paula Knight
Picture research: Erica Martin
Production: Duncan Gilbert

Origination by Chroma Graphics (Overseas) Pte Ltd
Printed and bound in China by South China Printing Co. Ltd

ISBN 978 0 431 18433 3 (hardback)
12 11 10 09 08
10 9 8 7 6 5 4 3 2 1

ISBN 978 0 431 18440 1 (paperback)
12 11 10 09 08
10 9 8 7 6 5 4 3 2 1

British Library Cataloguing in Publication Data
Barraclough, Sue
  Fire safety. - (Stay safe!)
  1. Fire prevention - Juvenile literature 2. Fires - Juvenile literature 3. Safety education - Juvenile literature
  I. Title
  363.3'77

Acknowledgements
The publishers would like to thank Robin Wilcox for assistance in the preparation of this book.

Every effort has been made to contact copyright holders of any material reproduced in this book. Any omissions will be rectified in subsequent printings if notice is given to the publishers.

Contents

Fire is useful.

Fire can hurt us, too.

Do you know how to stay safe
from fire?

Never play with matches or lighters.

Never use a cooker without a grown-up to help you.

Never throw your clothes over a lamp.
Your clothes might catch fire.

Always keep away from fires
or heaters.

Never panic if there is a fire.

Always have a plan.

Make sure you can get out quickly.

Never stop to pick up toys.
Never try to hide.

Never open a door if it is hot.
There might be fire on the other side.

Always stay low down.
There is less smoke there.

Always get out quickly and calmly.
Call 999 from a safe place.

Never run if your clothes catch fire.

Always stop, drop, and roll.
This puts the flames out.

Never go back inside until the fire
is out.

Always wait for the fire brigade to say it is safe.

Always remember fire can
be dangerous.

Always remember these fire safety rules and you will stay safe.

Fire safety rules

- Keep away from matches, lighters, fires, or heaters.
- Make sure you have a plan if there is a fire.
- Make sure you now how to get out.
- Get out quickly and calmly.
- Call 999.
- Stay low down to keep away from smoke.
- Stop, drop, and roll to put out flames.
- Wait until the fire brigade says it is safe to go back in.

Picture glossary

 **fire brigade** the people whose job is to put out fires

 **flames** the bright, flickering part of a fire that you can see

 **panic** be afraid and not think clearly

 **plan** idea of how to do something

Index

Notes for parents and teachers
Before reading
Discuss with the children the dangers of fires. Why is it dangerous to play with matches? Why is there a fire guard round a fire? Why do people have smoke alarms? Talk about the fire drill at school.
After reading
Fire safety poster. Design a poster with the children about keeping safe. Draw a picture of a fire in the centre and, around it, write down the suggestions that the children offer.
Fire history. Tell the children the story of the Great Fire of London in 1666. Explain how it started in Pudding Lane and spread because the houses were built of wood and they were very close together. Teach them the song "London's Burning".
Fire-fighter's song. To the tune of "I'm a Little Teapot," sing: "I'm a fire-fighter, (child's name) is my name, I wear a helmet when I put out the flames. When I see the fire, I give a shout, 'Come on, fire-fighters, put the fire out!'"